# Celebrate Easter

**Easy Dramas, Speeches, and Recitations for Children**

Abingdon Press

# CELEBRATE EASTER

Copyright © 2002 by Abingdon Press

All rights reserved.

Abingdon Press hereby grants permission to local churches to reproduce the material contained in this publication for purposes of rehearsal and performance, provided the following notice appears on each copy:

**Copyright © 2002 by Abingdon Press. All rights reserved.**

No further reproduction or distribution of this material is allowed without the written consent of Abingdon Press. Requests for permission should be submitted to: Abingdon Press, 201 Eighth Ave. South, Nashville, TN 37202, or faxed to 615-749-6128, or e-mailed to permissions@abingdonpress.com

ISBN 9780687026944

Unless otherwise noted, Scripture quotations are from the New Revised Standard Version of the Bible. Copyright © 1989 by the Division of Christian Education of the National Council of the Churches of Christ in the United States of America. Used by permission. All rights reserved.

"Hosanna! Alleluia!", "Do You Believe?" and "The Easter Story" by Alecia Glaize are copyright © 2001 by Cokesbury.

"Go and Tell" and "An Easter Litany" are adapted from *Exploring Faith: Older Elementary*, Spring 2001; copyright © 2000 by Cokesbury.

"Hosanna! Hosanna!" and "Sing for Joy" by Daphna Flegal are copyright © 1996 by Cokesbury.

"Jesus Rose," "What the Women Said," and "What Jesus Said" are adapted from *New Invitation: Grades 1–2*, Spring 1998; copyright © 1997 by Cokesbury.

"A Palm Sunday Prayer" is copyright © 1998 by Cokesbury.

08 09 10 11 — 10 9 8 7 6 5 4

PRINTED IN THE UNITED STATES OF AMERICA

# CONTENTS

Hosanna! Alleluia! ............................. 5
Sonrise! ......................................... 7
Do You Believe? ............................. .25
The Easter Story ............................. .27
Go and Tell .................................... .29
An Easter Litany ............................. .32
Easter Verses for Young Children ............... .33
Easter Verses for Younger Elementary Children ... .38
Mother's Day Verses ......................... .41
Father's Day Verses .......................... .43
It Is God Who Sends the Spring ............... .44
Birds Singing in the Tree Tops ................ .45
Symbols of Lent and Easter ................... .46

# *HOSANNA! ALLELUIA!*
## Alecia Glaize

### **Production Notes**

*This reader's theatre piece can be done using children in grades three and up. It is perfect for involving the whole Sunday school. If used in a worship setting, involve the whole congregation as the Crowd. Children can wear either their Sunday best or biblical costumes.*

### **Characters**

Readers 1–4    Jesus    Crowd

**READER 1:** When Jesus and his disciples had come near Jerusalem, Jesus sent two of his disciples ahead.

**JESUS:** Go into the village ahead. There you will find a donkey and her colt. Untie them and bring them to me. If anyone asks you what you are doing, say, "The Lord needs them."

**READER 2:** Jesus did this for a special reason. Long ago a prophet had written, "Look, your king is coming to you, humble and riding on a donkey."

**READER 3:** The disciples did as Jesus had told them. They brought the donkey and the colt to Jesus. Then they put their cloaks on the donkey, and Jesus sat on it.

**READER 4:** A king riding on a donkey and not on a horse? What kind of king is this?

**READER 1:** It is a king who comes in peace, not war. Look. See how the people greet him.

**CROWD:** Hosanna! Alleluia!
Hear the people sing!
Hosanna! Alleluia!
Loud praises to our king!

**LEADER 2:** The crowd spread their cloaks on the road for the donkey and her colt to walk upon. Some cut branches from the trees and spread them on the road ahead.

**CROWD:** Hosanna! Alleluia!
Hear the people sing!
Hosanna! Alleluia!
Loud praises to our king!

**READER 3:** The people called Jesus the Son of David. They called him blessed.

**CROWD:** Hosanna! Alleluia!
Hear the people sing!
Hosanna! Alleluia!
Loud praises to our king!

**READER 4:** When Jesus entered the city, everyone was excited. "Who is this?" they asked one another.

**READER 1:** It is Jesus of Nazareth, the prophet from Galilee.

**CROWD:** Hosanna! Alleluia!
Hear the people sing!
Hosanna! Alleluia!
Loud praises to our king!
(Based on Matthew 21:1-11)

The End

# SONRISE!
## Gail Kittleson

### Production Notes

*This play is written with middle-school students in mind, but it can also include younger children in the Chorus. The scenery can be made by the participants, mostly out of cardboard boxes and paint.*

*Some type of speaker system is vital—the conversations are the content of the play.*

*The Chorus can have as many or as few children as you have in your congregation or Sunday school. The Chorus may wear robes or Sunday clothes. These participants should stand near the stage or in one corner of the stage. For a very small group, you may choose to have the choral solos be recited by the entire Chorus.*

### Characters

| | | |
|---|---|---|
| Chorus | Joseph | Soldier 1 |
| Greeter | Nicodemus | Soldier 2 |
| Guard | Mary | Soldier 3 |
| Servant | Salome | Andrew |
| Girl 1 | Joanna | Angel |
| Girl 2 | John | Guards |
| Peter | Philip | Servants |
| Jesus | Mary Magdalene | |

**Greeter:** We welcome you to our play, "Sonrise!" Just as the sun rises every morning, Jesus, God's only son, rose from the dead. Because Jesus died for our sins, we can be forgiven. Peter, Jesus' disciple, learned this lesson the hard way. In our play you will see how discouraged Peter was after he denied Jesus. That's the bad news—but the good news is that Peter found out that Jesus will forgive us even when we have trouble forgiving ourselves!

### Scene One: Late Thursday night
<u>Set</u>: *Courtyard of high priest's palace.*

*A few* GUARDS *and* SERVANTS *from the palace are huddled around a fire.*

**Guard:** *(Walking up to group)* It's cold tonight. Move over, friend. Let me get by the fire.

*The group makes room for the new arrival.* PETER *enters and walks toward the fire.*

**Servant:** I wonder what's going on inside now at the trial?

**Guard:** The chief priest has more witnesses testifying against Jesus.

GUARD *moves over to let* PETER *sit down.*

**Girl 1:** I wish they'd hurry. I'm so tired. *(Points at* PETER *and whispers loudly to the others)* Hey! Isn't this man one of Jesus' followers?

**Peter:** No, not me! You must have me mixed up with someone else. *(Laughs nervously)*

**GUARD:** When will the trial be over? It's almost morning.

**SERVANT:** At this rate, we'll never get any sleep.

**GIRL 2:** Don't worry—it's almost over. And you can bet that by the sabbath this Jesus will be convicted and crucified. *(Pauses and points at* PETER*)* You must be one of Jesus' followers. I think I've seen you with him!

**PETER:** I am not! I don't even know him!

**SERVANT:** But you're from Galilee, just like Jesus.

PETER *jumps up and backs away from the group, speaking angrily.*

**PETER:** So what? That doesn't prove I'm his follower. I tell you, I don't know him!

*A rooster crows loudly three times.* PETER *looks off-stage horror-stricken. The others follow his gaze.*

**GIRL 1:** *(Pointing in the other direction)* Look! They're taking Jesus away now. Poor man!

*Overcome with shame,* PETER *runs offstage, down an aisle or through audience, if possible.*

**SERVANT:** What's got into him?

**GUARD:** Who knows? Come on—let's go.

*Everyone exits.*

## **Scene Two:** **Friday morning**

PETER *runs wildly back up the aisle onto the stage, slumping to the floor, hands over his face, sobbing.*

**CHORUS:** I have denied my Lord!
What shall I do?
Where can I run?
Jesus, my friend—
Jesus, God's Son!

**SOLO VOICE:** What are you doing here?

**PETER:** *(Defensive, holding his hands out)* I'm hiding, that's what. Don't you know Jesus was arrested last night? They could get me too.

**SOLO VOICE:** YOU said you weren't Jesus' disciple.

**SOLO VOICE:** YOU denied him three times!

PETER *covers his face in shame.*

**SOLO VOICE:** YOU ran away and let Jesus die alone.

PETER *looks up at the* CHORUS *in shocked surprise.*

**PETER:** Is Jesus . . . dead?

**Chorus:** *(Slowly, quietly)* Yes. He's dying, dying. And you ran away and let him die alone! Why weren't you there, Peter?

PETER *again hides his face, shaking his head in great agitation.*

**Solo Voice:** *(Mocking)* He's scared!

**Solo Voice:** Peter's scared!

**Solo Voice:** He's scared the soldiers will come for him too.

**Solo Voice:** He's blaming himself. He's confused.

**Chorus:** But most of all, he's scared!

**Chorus:** They are killing my best friend!
Will this awful day ever end?
And I've been unfaithful too!
Now, what will I ever do?
I never want to leave this place,
For now my life is pure disgrace.
And I am feeling very sad—
They've killed my Lord.
It's worse than bad.

## Scene Three: Late Friday afternoon
### Set: *The tomb.*

JOSEPH *and* NICODEMUS *solemnly carry the body of* JESUS, *wrapped in a white sheet, across the stage. They disappear through the door of the tomb. The women follow behind and sit nearby, weeping.*

JOSEPH *and* NICODEMUS *come out of the tomb.*

**JOSEPH:** Why, oh, why did they have to kill Jesus? I was sure he was the Messiah.

**NICODEMUS:** I'm so glad you had a tomb to bury him in. We won't have time to finish preparing his body.

**MARY:** Can we help?

**JOSEPH:** Not now. It's almost the sabbath, and we must go home.

NICODEMUS *and* JOSEPH *put the stone in front of the tomb door with great effort.*

**NICODEMUS:** Are you coming too?

**MARY:** Yes, in a few minutes.

NICODEMUS *and* JOSEPH *exit.*

**SALOME:** Isn't there something we can do, Mary?

MARY: We can't do anything now. But we can come back here after the sabbath's over and put spices on Jesus' body.

JOANNA: Do you think it's safe?

SALOME: They might arrest us.

MARY: I don't know—maybe you're right. Let's go home now, and we can decide what to do.

MARY, SALOME, *and* JOANNA *exit.*

## Scene Four: Saturday and early Sunday
Set: *The tomb.*

### Production Notes

*For extra dramatic effect, add rumbling sheet metal and some "smoke" from blowing flour to simulate the earthquake.*

*Several* **SOLDIERS** *march in and stand guard at the tomb door. One* **SOLDIER** *fastens the Roman seal to the tomb, and the others secure the area. They stand guard for a few minutes. Suddenly the* **SOLDIERS** *begin to rock back and forth and drum their spears on the floor. They are terrified.*

**SOLDIER 1:** Listen to that thunder! A big storm is coming!

**SOLDIER 2:** What's going on? It must be an earthquake!

**SOLDIER 3:** An earthquake? How can that be?

**SOLDIER 2:** I don't know, but let's get out of here!

*They suddenly fall to the ground as though unconscious. An* ANGEL *enters and moves the stone blocking the tomb door to one side, leaving the entrance open. The* **SOLDIERS**, *who are just coming to, see the* ANGEL.

**SOLDIER 1:** Yikes! Who is that?

*He runs offstage in fright.*

**SOLDIER 2:** It's a ghost!

*He crawls offstage, frantically trying to get away.*

## Scene Five

<u>Set</u>: *A room with a low table with some food. There is a door on the side from which Peter will enter.*

JOHN, ANDREW, *and* PHILIP *are sitting at the table.* PETER *steals onstage, looking all around as if afraid someone if following him. He knocks at a door, waits, and knocks again, a little louder.*

JOHN *comes out, rubbing his eyes and stretching. He sees* PETER *and grabs him.*

**JOHN:** Come in! Where in the world have you been?

**PETER:** Shh, not so loud. Someone might hear us. *(Looks around)* Hello, Andrew. Hi, Philip. Have the others been arrested?

**JOHN:** No, they're up on the roof sleeping. You must be hungry. Come on over here and sit down.

*They cross the stage;* JOHN *picks up some food from the table and places it in front of* PETER *as* PETER *sits down.*

**PETER:** Thanks, John. I'm starved.

**ANDREW:** Why haven't you come here sooner? We've all been so worried about you!

PETER *stops eating and looks upset.*

**PHILIP:** We were afraid you'd been arrested, Peter.

**PETER:** *(Sighing)* No, I've been . . . staying by myself. *(Sighing deeply again)* I just couldn't face you all.

ANDREW: What are you talking about?

PETER: After Judas betrayed Jesus, I betrayed Jesus too. I went to the high priest's house to find out what they were going to do to Jesus. When someone asked me if I was Jesus' follower, I said, "No!"

ANDREW *sympathetically puts his hand on* PETER's *shoulder.*

ANDREW: You were just scared, Peter.

PETER: That's no excuse! It happened three times! THREE times. I don't deserve to be called Jesus' disciple ever again.

PETER *puts head in hands.*

PHILIP: I know you feel terrible, but I think Jesus would understand. He wouldn't hold it against you. He just wasn't like that.

PETER: I'd hold it against him if he'd done that to me.

PHILIP: Peter, don't you remember that Jesus warned us we would all run away and let him suffer and die alone? And when you insisted that you'd rather die and do that, Jesus said . . .

PETER: *(Interrupting)*: I remember. He said I'd disown him three times. *(Jumping up)* But I still can't believe I did it!

**JOHN:** *(Pausing, then getting up)* You're no more guilty than the rest of us. We've all let Jesus down.

**PETER:** I suppose so. What makes me feel so bad is that I'll never be able to make it up to him. Never. If only Jesus were alive again. *(The others nod and sigh.)* If only I could tell him I loved him one more time. *(Pausing)* What's the use? It's all over, John— everything we've been counting on.

**JOHN:** All we can do is wait and see what happens. You look so tired, Peter. Come. We both need some sleep.

*They all exit.*

**CHORUS:** Sleep? It's impossible!
How can he sleep?
He's lost his best friend,
He can only weep.
Tired, yes, so tired,
But his mind won't be quiet;
If he could think of something
To do now, he'd try it.

## **Scene Six: Early Sunday morning**
<u>Set</u>: *Mary's house.*

MARY *is alone onstage. She puts on her sandals and wraps a shawl around her head, getting ready to go outside. She picks up a jar of spices and paces back and forth, holding the jar.*

*Begin with the* CHORUS *and* MARY *alternately speaking their parts in rhythm. Choral parts may be spoken by the whole group in unison, by a soloist, or by small groups. Or you may prefer to have the* CHORUS *speak all its parts first, followed by* MARY*'s answer.*

**CHORUS:** Mary, Mary, what's the matter?
Why are you so upset?
Where are you going so early?
You shouldn't be up yet!

**MARY:** I have to go and find my Lord,
And put these spices on—
His body need to be embalmed,
He is, you know, God's son!

**CHORUS:** But Mary, think! This plan won't work,
Besides, it's dangerous!
Jesus is dead now, just stay home—
Be safe, don't make a fuss!

**MARY:** I cannot just stay inside and fret,
I must find something to do.
Jesus did so much for me;
Am I a friend that's true?

**Chorus:** There's no way you can move that stone.
Why don't you stop and think?
It's still so very dark outside—
The sky is not yet pink.

**Mary:** But it's my Lord there in that tomb,
And he is all alone;
I love him, and I want to help.
Somehow I'll move that stone!

MARY *exits.*

## Scene Seven: A little later on Sunday.
Set: *The tomb.*

SALOME, MARY, *and* JOANNA *are talking as they approach the tomb. The entrance to the tomb is open, but they do not notice this right away.*

**SALOME:** Ohhh, I wonder who will help us move the stone away from in front of the door?

**MARY:** Look! *(Pointing excitedly)* The guards have gone!

**SALOME:** *(Gasping)* The stone!

**JOANNA:** It's rolled away. You don't suppose someone has broken into the tomb?

*The women rush forward to look into the tomb. As they step back in surprise, the* ANGEL *stands in the entrance. The women cling to one another in fright, looking as if they might faint.*

**ANGEL:** Don't be afraid. I know you're looking for Jesus. But he is not here. He has risen from the dead, just as he said he would. Look, here is where he was lying.

*The* ANGEL *points inside the tomb. The women lean forward a little as if to look into the tomb, but they are too frightened to move.*

**ANGEL:** Go quickly! Tell Peter and the disciples that Jesus has risen from the dead and will see them soon!

*The* ANGEL *steps back into the tomb. The* CHORUS *sings a verse of any Easter song that is familiar to your church. The women look at one another in confusion and fear, then excitement. They hurry offstage.*

## Scene Eight

<u>Set</u>: *Back in the room where Peter and the other disciples are staying.*

**JOHN:** Come on, Mary. You don't expect us to believe that!

**PETER:** You've been dreaming.

**SALOME:** It's true, John and Peter. We saw an angel!

**JOANNA:** And the angel said that Jesus is alive!

**MARY:** The angel said to tell the disciples and you, Peter.

**PETER:** Me? The angel mentioned me?

**ANDREW:** Look, there's no way Jesus could've gotten out of the tomb. The guards were there, and the stone—

**JOHN:** How could he have escaped?

**PETER:** *(Interrupting)* I'm going to the tomb, John.

**PHILIP:** Peter, why waste your time? This story can't be true!

**PETER:** Mary said the angel mentioned me. Maybe I've still got a chance!

**JOHN:** I'm coming with you!

*The* DISCIPLES *exit.* PETER *and* JOHN *run down the aisle.*

## Scene Nine
<u>Set</u>: *The tomb.*

JOHN, PETER, *and the other* DISCIPLES *rush in.*

**JOHN:** I don't see any angel.

**PETER:** But Jesus isn't here, either.

**JOHN:** Peter, do you remember when Jesus told us he would come alive after three days?

**PETER:** *(Nodding)* I didn't understand what he meant then. *(Pauses; becomes excited.)* Oh, John, do you think Jesus really could be alive?

**JOHN:** *(Thoughtfully)* The women seemed so sure— *(Shakes head in wonder).* It seems impossible, yet I remember what he said . . .

**PETER:** *(Sighs)* I don't know what to believe. What's the use thinking about it?

MARY MAGDALENE *runs in, very excited and happy.*

**MARY MAGDALENE:** Jesus really is alive! I saw him myself!

**JOHN:** Are you sure about this?

**MARY**
**MAGDALENE:** Positively sure. He even talked to me!

**PETER:** When did you see him? What did he say to you?

**MARY**
**MAGDALENE:** I thought he was the gardener. I saw him at the tomb and asked where he'd taken Jesus—and then he said my name, and . . . and . . . oh, it was so exciting! I even touched him. Oh, there's no doubt in my mind . . . I don't understand, but I know it's true.

**PETER:** Whew! I don't understand it, either. But then, there were a lot of times when I didn't understand what was going on with Jesus. I think maybe Jesus *is* alive!

**JOHN:** I believe it too. This changes everything!

*The other disciples murmur excitedly to one another.*

**CHORUS:** Yes! He's alive! Jesus is risen from the dead!

**SOLO VOICE:** You'll see Jesus soon! He still loves you, Peter!

**SOLO VOICE:** He will forgive you for denying him and running away.

**SOLO VOICE:** And Jesus will send you into all the world to tell the good news!

**SOLO VOICE:** Soon you will be telling others how they can be forgiven!

**SOLO VOICE:** He will give you power, and he will stay with you forever.

**CHORUS:** For God so loved the world that he gave his only Son, so that everyone who believes in him may not perish but may have eternal life. (John 3:16)

The End

# *DO YOU BELIEVE?*
Alecia Glaize

**GROUP 1:** One day the followers of Jesus
Were feeling quite sad and distressed.
Their longtime friend and their teacher
Had died a most terrible death.
The man they knew then as Jesus,
The Messiah, the Savior, God's Son,
No longer walked right beside them.
They feared that his message was done.

**GROUP 2:** But Jesus had promised his followers,
On the third day he'd be raised from the dead,
So they buried him there in the garden,
And God raised him just as he'd said.
When the Marys came to attend him,
The stone had been rolled away.
And an angel as bright as the lightning
Said, "He is risen on this very day."

**GROUP 3:** Word of the miracle soon traveled.
You can't keep a good rumor down.
"Jesus is truly the Messiah!"
Was the word that went all over town.
Some women had heard Jesus talking.
With some Jesus had shared a good meal.
At one time he held out his hands,
And invited his disciples to feel.

**GROUP 4:** But one of his disciples named Thomas
Said, "I just can't believe that it's true.
Jesus alive? Never happened!
Whatever you say or you do!
To convince me then show me the nail prints,
And place my hand on his side.
Till then call me Thomas the doubtful.
Personally, I think that somebody lied."

**GROUP 1:** Then something happened one evening,
As all the disciples came 'round.
And this time Thomas was with them,
But he just stood there and made not a sound.
"Peace be with you," Jesus said to them,
Then he beckoned that Thomas come near.
"Touch my hands and my side," Jesus told him.
"You have no reason to fear."

**GROUP 2:** Thomas stood there just like a statue.
He didn't wiggle or jiggle or nod.
But these are the words that came out of his mouth,
"You are my Lord and my God."
Then Jesus smiled in a sad way,
"I know you believe 'cause you've seen.
How blessed are those among you
Who believe but have never yet seen."

(Based on John 20:19-29)

The End

# THE EASTER STORY
## Alecia Glaize

### Production Notes

*This is a simple Easter drama for middle elementary students and up. The only prop needed is the large stone. Use lighting to convey the changing time.*

### Characters

| | | |
|---|---|---|
| Narrator | Mary Magdalene | Mary, the mother of James |
| Salome | Angel | |

**NARRATOR:** It was early morning. The sabbath was over. Mary Magdalene, Mary the mother of James, and Salome made their way toward the garden where Jesus was buried.

**MARY MAGDALENE:** I can't believe all that has happened. Who would have believed it?

**MARY:** We didn't even have time to prepare his body and show the proper respect.

**SALOME:** I wonder who will roll the stone away so that we can get in. It's a very big stone, you know.

**NARRATOR:** The three women entered the garden and stopped immediately.

**MARY MAGDALENE:** Look! The stone has already been rolled away!

**MARY:** Do you think someone has taken Jesus away?

**SALOME:** Where would they put him? What will the others say?

**NARRATOR:** The three women stepped inside the tomb and were surprised to find a young man sitting where Jesus' body had been placed just three days ago.

**MARY MAGDALENE:** Who are you? Where did you come from?

**MARY:** Where is Jesus? Where did you put him?

**ANGEL:** Don't be afraid. You are looking for Jesus of Nazareth. He's not here. He has been raised. Look, this is the place where they put him. He is going ahead of you to Galilee. There you will see him just as he told you.

**NARRATOR:** The three women ran from the tomb. They were afraid to tell anyone what had happened.

**SALOME:** No one will believe us!

**MARY MAGDALENE:** I can't believe it myself.

**NARRATOR:** But soon the word got out. Jesus appeared to Mary Magdalene and to the other disciples. Jesus was alive! God had raised him from the dead, just as Jesus had said God would do.

(Based on Mark 16:1-8)

## The End

# GO AND TELL

## Production Notes

*Present this short drama with very few props—just the suggestion of a house on one side of the stage, with a door that opens. Peter and two other disciples are "inside" the house as the women enter. When they leave to go find Jesus, the women will exit into the house.*

## Characters

Narrator  
Peter  
Mary  
Mary Magdalene  
Jesus  
Disciple 2  
Disciple 3

**NARRATOR:** We are an Easter people. The story of Jesus' resurrection didn't stop on Easter morning. He appeared to many of his followers in the days following Easter, and he had something to say to them, something that he wanted them to do; and he tells us the same thing now. Listen:

On the first day of the week, the disciples were together in a house, hiding for fear that the authorities might come after them and punish them for being followers of Jesus. But Mary Magdalene and the other Mary left before sunrise to finish the ritual for the burial of Jesus' body. Just after sunrise, they came back.

MARY MAGDALENE *and* MARY *run in and excitedly knock on the door of the house. They are both out of breath.*

**PETER:** (*From inside the house*) Who is it?

**MARY MAGDALENE:** Hurry, Peter, open the door!

PETER *opens the door cautiously and steps outside.*

**PETER:** What's the matter? What happened?

**MARY:** Something amazing has happened! Jesus is not dead!

**PETER:** What are you saying? We saw him crucified. We saw his body laid in the tomb. Jesus is definitely not among the living.

**MARY MAGDALENE:** But wait, listen to what we have to say. We went to the tomb to prepare the body, but when we arrived, the stone had been rolled away and the tomb was empty. An angel appeared and told us that Jesus has been raised from the dead. He is alive and is waiting for all of you in Galilee.

**PETER:** What do you mean, he is alive? Maybe one of the Romans stole his body. What you are saying is impossible.

**MARY:** I agree. I don't know if I would believe it either if I hadn't seen him.

**PETER:** Who? Seen who?

**MARY:** Jesus! As we ran from the tomb, suddenly Jesus met us. It was really him!

**MARY MAGDALENE:** We fell down at his feet and thanked God. Then Jesus said, "Don't be afraid! Tell my followers to go to Galilee. They will see me there."

| | |
|---|---|
| **MARY:** | And we ran here to tell you that we must go immediately to Galilee. |

*The three disciples start across the stage.* MARY *and* MARY MAGDALENE *enter the house and close the door.* JESUS *enters from the other side. If possible, a spotlight should shine on him.*

| | |
|---|---|
| **NARRATOR:** | So the disciples immediately left the house and quickly traveled to a mountain in Galilee. And there was Jesus! When they saw him, they ran to meet him and worshiped him. |

*Disciples kneel at* JESUS' *feet.*

| | |
|---|---|
| **JESUS:** | All authority in heaven and on earth has been given to me. Go therefore and make disciples of all nations, baptizing them in the name of the Father and of the Son and of the Holy Spirit, and teaching them to obey everything that I have commanded you. And remember, I am with you always, to the end of the age. (Matthew 28:18-20) |

JESUS *exits.*

| | |
|---|---|
| **NARRATOR:** | As the disciples returned to Jerusalem, they kept repeating those words. |
| **PETER:** | Jesus is not dead, but is alive, and he is with us. |
| **DISCIPLE 2:** | We are supposed to go and make disciples. |
| **DISCIPLE 3:** | And remember, Jesus is always with us. |

The End

# An Easter Litany

**All:** This is a day of new beginnings!

**Reader 1:** Jesus was crucified on a cross and buried in a tomb.

**All:** This is a day of new beginnings!

**Reader 2:** As Mary Magdalene and the other Mary went to the tomb, they were very sad.

**All:** This is a day of new beginnings!

**Reader 3:** The angel said, "Jesus is not dead; he has been raised!'

**All:** This is a day of new beginnings!

**Reader 4:** Their sadness turned to joy. Could Jesus really be alive?

**All:** This is a day of new beginnings!

**Reader 5:** Suddenly, they saw Jesus. The tomb was empty! He is risen! Alleluia!

**All:** This is a day of new beginnings!

**Reader 6:** This is a day to leave our hurts and fears at the tomb and to know that Jesus is with us today.

**All:** This is a day of new beginnings! Alleluia!

# EASTER VERSES FOR YOUNG CHILDREN

## *Special Day*

What is the donkey thinking
On this special day?

Why is he so quiet and gentle?
Why doesn't he bray?

Why doesn't he buck and try
To break away and run?

Well, it's because of Jesus.
Jesus is so kind.

That even the donkey wants
To do his best to mind.

Jesus love the children,
And he loves animals too.

That's why we praise you, Jesus,
And listen and follow you!

*Gail Kittleson*

## *Palm Sunday*

We give our praise to Jesus
As we watch him ride along,
We shout our thanks with all our friends
And sing to him a song.
So many people are in this crowd!
So many people all shouting so loud!
Jesus will always be our friend.
We will praise him to the end.

*Gail Kittleson*

### *Hosanna! Hosanna!*

Hosanna! Hosanna!
*(Wave palm branches.)*
It's Palm Sunday today.
*(Brush palm branches on the floor.)*
We wave our palm branches
*(Wave palm branches.)*
And happily say,
*(Turn around.)*
"Hosanna! Hosanna!"
*(Wave palm branches.)*

"Hosanna! Hosanna!"
*(Wave palm branches.)*
It's Palm Sunday today.
*(Brush palm branches on the floor.)*
We hear stories of Jesus
*(Wave palm branches.)*
And happily say,
*(Turn around.)*
"Hosanna! Hosanna!"
*(Wave palm branches around.)*

*Daphna Flegal*

## *Sing for Joy*

Teach the children the sign for the word *joy*—hold hands in front of your chest, palms toward you, and move them upwards quickly. Let the children sign the word *joy* each time they say it.

>Joy, joy, joy,
>Joy to the Lord.
>Joy, joy, joy.
>
>We sing for Easter.
>It's a special day.
>A day to be happy,
>We sign, sing, and say,
>
>Joy, joy, joy,
>Joy to the Lord.
>Joy, joy, joy.
>
>We sing for Jesus,
>On this special day.
>Jesus is risen,
>We sign, sing, and say,
>
>Joy, joy, joy,
>Joy to the Lord.
>Joy, joy, joy.
>
>We sing for new life,
>On this special day.
>God plans for springtime.
>We sign, sing, and say,

Joy, joy, joy,
Joy to the Lord.
Joy, joy, joy.

We sing for God's love,
On this special day.
We know God loves us,
We sign, sing, and say,

Joy, joy, joy,
Joy to the Lord.
Joy, joy, joy.

*Daphna Flegal*

# Easter Verses for Younger Elementary Children

## A Parade Is a Good Thing

This is such a special day:
Mother says Jesus is coming this way!

Grandma says, "Now, children, come along, come!"
In the distance I hear a hum.

Father has spread his coat on the ground.
A donkey is coming—what is that sound?

People are shouting and cheering out loud.
What is the meaning of this big crowd?

Hosanna to him who comes in God's name,
Blessed is Jesus—the one who came.

They're worshiping him and singing psalms,
Shouting, laughing, and waving palms.

We know that this means he is the King;
That's the meaning of everything.

*Gail Kittleson*

## *Jesus Rose*

Jesus rose from the dead.
He appeared to his disciples and said,
"Go teach others what I taught you,
Love your God; love others too."

## *What the Women Said*

"The tomb is empty!" the women said.
God has raised Jesus from the dead.

## *What Jesus Said*

Dying on a cross, God's beloved Son
Said, "Forgive them, Father,
They don't know what they've done."

# A Palm Sunday Prayer

**Child 1:** Dear God, we remember that Jesus rode a donkey into Jerusalem. Together we say . . .

**All:** Hosanna!

**Child 2:** We give thanks for Jesus, who loved all people. Together we say . . .

**All:** Hosanna!

**Child 3:** We celebrate Jesus, the King! Together we say . . .

**All:** Hosanna!

**Child 1:** Hosanna and Amen!

# Mother's Day Verses

### To Mom With Love

Sometimes I think there just couldn't be
Anyone of earth as lucky as me;
I've got a mom who cares a lot,
And I'm so thankful for what I've got!
Happy Mother's Day!

*Gail Kittleson*


### Thanks, Mom

Through my growing-up years
You gave me pleasant memories
That come back to me in waves
Like flowery scents on an evening breeze.
Thanks, Mom.
Happy Mother's Day!

*Gail Kittleson*


### For My Mom

You bring sunshine in with you,
You shut the darkness out;
You are a bright spot in my world,
Of that there is no doubt!
May you have a Mother's Day that is just like you!

*Gail Kittleson*

### *On Mother's Day*

There is so much
To thank you for;
The older I grow,
I see it more.

A mother's love
Knows how to give,
And teaches her children
How to live.

I'm grateful, Mom,
On this special day;
You've brought so much
Good my way.

So thank you, Mom,
For all you've done.
I'll always be
The grateful one.

*Gail Kittleson*

# FATHER'S DAY VERSES

## Fathers Are For

Fathers are
For scraped-up knees,
Hearing tall tales,
Getting cats out of trees.

Fathers are
For hugs and love,
The best gift
From our Father above!

*Gail Kittleson*

## On Father's Day

On Father's Day
And all days thereafter,
May your life be filled
With love and laughter!

*Gail Kittleson*

## A Good Teacher

Those who have an earthly father
Who teaches them much about
Our Father in Heaven are the
Most blessed people on earth.

Thanks to you, Dad, I am one of those people.

*Gail Kittleson*

## *It Is God Who Sends the Spring*

I'm very glad the spring has come,
The sun shines out so bright;
The little birds upon the trees,
Are singing with delight.

I love to see the pretty flowers
That rain and sunshine bring;
When all things seem just like myself,
So glad to see the spring.

God must be very good indeed,
Who made each pretty thing;
For flowers and birds and sunshine say
It is God who sends the spring.

*Ida F. Leyda*

## *Birds Singing in the Tree Tops*

Birds singing in the tree tops,
Flowers blooming in the grass,
Close by the shady pathways,
Where little children pass.

Clouds floating high above us,
Boats sailing out to sea,
Far from the sandy seashore,
Where children love to be.

Hill, mountain, field, and valley,
Each one in beauty dressed;
And all the spreading shade trees.
Where children love to rest.

These all make happy summer,
God's gift—the great outdoors;
God made the trees and flowers,
The sea and sandy shores.

*Ida F. Leyda*

# Symbols of Lent and Easter

*Encourage the children to make posters or to cut out pictures of the symbols to hold up as they speak. If you have a number of very young children who are too young for speeches, you might let them hold up the symbols while an older child or older children tell about the symbol.*

**Child 1:** My symbol is the butterfly. The butterfly has become a symbol for Jesus' resurrection. A butterfly begins as an egg. Then it becomes a larvae, a caterpillar, a cocoon, and finally a butterfly.

A butterfly totally changes from one kind of creature to another. When we love and follow Jesus, we change too.

**Child 2:** My symbol is a pretzel. It is usually associated with the forty days before Easter that we know as Lent. A tradition that began during those days was to eat bread shaped to look like little arms crossed in prayer. They called the bread *bracelae*, which means "little arms." In other parts of the world, people called it *bretzel*, which later became *pretzel*.

Now people eat pretzels all year long. The next time you are having a snack of pretzels, say a prayer for the people of the world who have no food.

**CHILD 3:** My symbol is new clothing. Many new believers were baptized at Easter. They were given new white robes to celebrate their new life in Christ.

Now people buy new clothing to wear on Easter morning to remind themselves that just as Jesus rose to new life, we have a new life when we give our hearts to Jesus.

**CHILD 4:** My symbol is spring flowers. Like the new clothes that people put on for Easter, the earth has beautiful new clothing each spring.

As we look at the flowers, we remember that Jesus gave us new life too.

**CHILD 5:** My symbol is the Easter egg. During Lent people in the early church did not eat eggs. But the chickens kept laying them anyway. So when Easter came, there were lots of eggs to use.

Kings gave specially decorated eggs to their subjects. People painted eggs and gave them to children. When you make and play with Easter eggs, remember that the greatest gift of all was Jesus.